To:

_____

From:

_____

Date:

_____

Message:

_____

_____

_____

 S0-CFV-188

THE POWER OF A PRAYING® PARENT

BOOK OF PRAYERS

STORMIE OMARTIAN

HARVEST HOUSE PUBLISHERS

EUGENE, OREGON

All Scripture verses are taken from the New King James Version, Copyright © 1979, 1980, 1982 by Thomas Nelson, Inc., Publishers. Used by permission.

Cover by Koechel Peterson & Associates, Inc., Minneapolis, Minnesota

THE POWER OF A PRAYING is a registered trademark of The Hawkins Children's LLC. Harvest House Publishers, Inc., is the exclusive licensee of the federally registered trademark THE POWER OF A PRAYING.

THE POWER OF A PRAYING® PARENT BOOK OF PRAYERS
Copyright © 2004 by Stormie Omartian
Published by Harvest House Publishers
Eugene, Oregon 97402
www.harvesthousepublishers.com

ISBN-13: 978-0-7369-1706-3
ISBN-10: 0-7369-1706-3
Product # 6917063

All rights reserved. No part of this publication may be reproduced, stored in a retrieval system, or transmitted in any form or by any means— electronic, mechanical, digital, photocopy, recording, or any other—except for brief quotations in printed reviews, without the prior permission of the publisher.

Printed in the United States of America

06 07 08 09 10 11 /VP-KB/ 10 9 8 7 6 5 4 3

Introduction

"I don't know how to be the perfect parent for my children," I said to God in desperation one day. "I need You to help me raise them."

God responded by impressing on my heart the following words: *If you are not covering your children in prayer every day, you are leaving their lives to chance.*

What a frightening thought!

"Then teach me how to pray for my children the way You would have me to, Lord," I said.

Over the next few years, I learned how to cover every aspect of my children's lives in prayer. I also learned that I didn't have to be a *perfect* parent; I just had to be a *praying* parent. That was something I *could* do.

For the past 25 years I have been praying for my children (yes, they are now grown, and I'm still praying), and I have seen such wonderful answers to my prayers.

Throughout that time I've had regular prayer groups in my home for the sole purpose of praying for the children of everyone who attended. Each one of the participants has seen countless answers to prayer as well. That's because prayer works! And there is no more powerful prayer than that of a parent for his or her child.

God has given you spiritual authority over your child, and your prayers have power. This doesn't mean there will always be an immediate answer. Sometimes it can take days, weeks, months, or even years. But *your prayers are never meaningless.* If you are praying, something is happening.

I hope this book will be a helpful reminder to keep your children covered in prayer. I know you'll agree that leaving their lives to chance is not good enough.

– Stormie Omartian –

*All your children shall be taught by the L<small>ORD</small>,
and great shall be the peace of your children.*

Isaiah 54:13

Becoming a Praying Parent

Lord, I submit myself to You. I realize that parenting a child in the way You would have me to is beyond my human abilities. I know I need You to help me. I want to partner with You and partake of Your gifts of wisdom, discernment, revelation, and guidance. I also need Your strength and patience, along with a generous portion of Your love flowing through me.

Teach me how to love the way You love. Where I need to be healed, delivered, changed, matured, or made whole, I invite You to do that in me. Help me to walk in righteousness and integrity before You.

Teach me Your ways, enable me to obey Your commandments and do only what is pleasing in Your sight.

The righteous man walks in his integrity; his children are blessed after him.

Proverbs 20:7

Prayer Notes

_____

_____

_____

_____

_____

_____

_____

_____

_____

_____

_____

Becoming a Praying Parent

Lord, may the beauty of Your Spirit be so evident in me that I will be a godly role model for my child. Give me the communication, teaching, and nurturing skills that I must have.

Grow me into being the kind of parent You want me to be and teach me how to pray and truly intercede for his (her) life. You said in Your Word, "Whatever things you ask in prayer, believing, you will receive" (Matthew 21:22).

In Jesus' name I ask that You will increase my faith to believe for all the things You have put on my heart to pray for concerning this child.

Whatever you ask in My name, that I will do,
that the Father may be glorified in the Son. If
you ask anything in My name, I will do it.

John 14:13-14

Prayer Notes

_____

_____

_____

_____

_____

_____

_____

_____

_____

_____

_____

Releasing My Child into God's Hands

Lord, I come to You in Jesus' name and give (name of child) to You. I'm convinced that You alone know what is best for him (her).

You alone know what he (she) needs. I release him (her) to You to care for and protect, and I commit myself to pray for everything concerning him (her) that I can think of or that You put upon my heart.

Teach me how to pray and guide me in what to pray about. Help me not to impose my own will when I'm praying for him (her), but rather enable me to pray that Your will be done in his (her) life. Thank You that I can partner with You in raising him (her) and that I don't have to do it alone.

The mercy of the LORD is from everlasting to everlasting on those who fear Him, and His righteousness to children's children, to such as keep His covenant, and to those who remember His commandments to do them.

Psalm 103:17-18

Prayer Notes

Releasing My Child into God's Hands

Thank You, Lord, for the precious gift of this child. Because Your Word says that every good gift comes from You, I know that You have given him (her) to me to care for and raise.

Help me to do that. Show me places where I continue to hang on to him (her) and enable me to release him (her) to Your protection, guidance, and counsel.

Help me not to live in fear of possible dangers, but in the joy and peace of knowing that You are in control. I'm grateful that I don't have to rely on the world's unreliable and everchanging methods of child rearing, but that I can have clear directions from Your Word and wisdom as I pray to You for answers. I rely on You for everything, and this day I trust my child to You and release him (her) into Your hands.

If you then, being evil, know how to give good gifts to your children, how much more will your Father who is in heaven give good things to those who ask Him!

Matthew 7:11

Prayer Notes

_____

_____

_____

_____

_____

_____

_____

_____

_____

Securing Protection from Harm

Lord, I lift (name of child) up to You and ask that You would put a hedge of protection around her (him). Protect her (his) spirit, body, mind, and emotions from any kind of evil or harm.

I pray specifically for protection from accidents, disease, injury, or any other physical, mental, or emotional abuse.

I pray that she (he) will make her (his) refuge "in the shadow of Your wings" until "these calamities have passed by" (Psalm 57:1).

Hide her (him) from any kind of evil influences that would come against her (him).

When you pass through the waters, I will be with you; and through the rivers, they shall not overflow you. When you walk through the fire, you shall not be burned, nor shall the flame scorch you.

Isaiah 43:2

Prayer Notes

_____

_____

_____

_____

_____

_____

_____

_____

_____

Securing Protection from Harm

Thank You, Lord, for Your many promises of protection. I pray that You will put a hedge of safety and protection around (name of child) on every side and keep her (him) away from harm.

Protect her (him) from any hidden dangers and let no weapon formed against her (him) be able to prosper.

Help her (him) to walk in Your ways and in obedience to Your will so that she (he) never comes out from under the umbrella of that protection.

Keep her (him) safe in all she (he) does and wherever she (he) goes. In Jesus' name, I pray.

Because you have made the LORD, who is my refuge, even the Most High, your dwelling place, no evil shall befall you, nor shall any plague come near your dwelling.

Psalm 91:9-10

Prayer Notes

Feeling Loved and Accepted

Lord, I pray for (name of child) to feel loved and accepted. Penetrate his (her) heart with Your love right now and help him (her) to fully understand how far-reaching and complete it is. Your Word says You loved us so much that You sent Your Son to die for us (John 3:16).

Deliver him (her) from any lies of the enemy that may have been planted in his (her) mind to cause him (her) to doubt that. Lord, help (name of child) to abide in Your love. May he (she) say as David did, "Cause me to hear Your loving-kindness in the morning, for in You do I trust" (Psalm 143:8).

Manifest Your love to this child in a real way today and help him (her) to receive it.

God is love, and he who abides in love abides in God, and God in him.

1 John 4:16

Prayer Notes

Feeling Loved and Accepted

Lord, I pray that You would help me to love this child unconditionally the way You do, and enable me to show it in a manner he (she) can perceive.

Reveal to me how I can demonstrate and model Your love to him (her) so that it will be clearly understood. I pray that all my family members will love and accept him (her), and may he (she) find favor with other people as well.

With each day that he (she) grows in the confidence of being loved and accepted, as he (she) comes to fully understand the depth of Your love for him (her), make him (her) a vessel through which Your love flows to others.

In Jesus' name I pray.

In this is love, not that we loved God, but that He loved us and sent His Son to be the propitiation for our sins. Beloved, if God so loved us, we also ought to love one another.

1 John 4:10-11

Prayer Notes

_____

_____

_____

_____

_____

_____

_____

_____

_____

Establishing an Eternal Future

Lord, I bring (name of child) before You and ask that You would help her (him) grow into a deep understanding of who You are.

Open her (his) heart and bring her (him) to a full knowledge of the truth about You. Lord, You have said in Your Word, "If you confess with your mouth the Lord Jesus and believe in your heart that God has raised Him from the dead, you will be saved" (Romans 10:9).

I pray for that kind of faith for my child. May she (he) call You her (his) Savior, be filled with Your Holy Spirit, acknowledge You in every area of her (his) life, and choose always to follow You and Your ways. Help her (him) to fully believe that Jesus laid down His life for her (him) so that she (he) might have life eternally and abundantly now.

This is the will of Him who sent Me, that everyone who sees the Son and believes in Him may have everlasting life; and I will raise him up at the last day.

John 6:40

Prayer Notes

_____

_____

_____

_____

_____

_____

_____

_____

_____

_____

Establishing an Eternal Future

Lord, I pray that (name of child) will live a fruitful life, ever increasing in the knowledge of You. May she (he) always know Your will, have spiritual understanding, and walk in a manner that is pleasing in Your sight. You have said in Your Word that You will pour out Your Spirit on my offspring (Isaiah 44:3).

I pray that You would pour out Your Spirit upon (name of child) this day. Help her (him) to comprehend the fullness of Your forgiveness so that she (he) will not live in guilt and condemnation.

Thank You, Lord, that You care about her (his) eternal future even more than I do and that it is secure in You.

In Jesus' name I pray that she (he) will not doubt or stray from the path You have for her (him) all the days of her (his) life.

I will pray the Father, and He will give you another Helper, that He may abide with you forever—the Spirit of truth, whom the world cannot receive, because it neither sees Him nor knows Him; but you know Him, for He dwells with you and will be in you.

John 14:16-17

Prayer Notes

_____

_____

_____

_____

_____

_____

_____

_____

_____

Honoring Parents and Resisting Rebellion

Lord, I pray that You would give (name of child) a heart that desires to obey You. Put into him (her) a longing to spend time with You, in Your Word and in prayer, listening for Your voice. Shine Your light upon any secret or unseen rebellion that is taking root in his (her) heart, so that it can be identified and destroyed.

Lord, I pray that he (she) will not give himself (herself) over to pride, selfishness, and rebellion, but that he (she) will be delivered from it. By the authority You've given me in Jesus' name, I "stand against the wiles of the devil" and I resist idolatry, rebellion, stubbornness, and disrespect; they will have no part in my son's (daughter's) life, nor will my child walk a path of destruction and death because of them.

The eye that mocks his father, and scorns obedience to his mother, the ravens of the valley will pick it out, and the young eagles will eat it.

Proverbs 30:17

Prayer Notes

_____

_____

_____

_____

_____

_____

_____

_____

_____

_____

Honoring Parents and Resisting Rebellion

Lord, Your Word instructs, "Children, obey your parents in all things, for this is well pleasing to the Lord" (Colossians 3:20).

I pray that You would turn the heart of (name of child) toward his (her) parents and enable him (her) to honor and obey both father and mother so that his (her) life will be long and good. Turn his (her) heart toward You so that all he (she) does is pleasing in Your sight.

May he (she) learn to identify and confront pride and rebellion in himself (herself) and be willing to confess and repent of it. Make him (her) uncomfortable with sin.

Help him (her) to know the beauty and simplicity of walking with a sweet and humble spirit in obedience and submission to You.

My son, hear the instruction of your father, and do not forsake the law of your mother; for they will be a graceful ornament on you head, and chains about your neck.

Proverbs 1:8-9

Prayer Notes

_____

_____

_____

_____

_____

_____

_____

_____

_____

Maintaining Good Family Relationships

Lord, I pray for (name of child) and her (his) relationship with all family members. Protect and preserve them from any unresolved or permanent breach.

Fill her (his) heart with Your love and give her (him) an abundance of compassion and forgiveness that will overflow to each member of the family.

Specifically, I pray for a close, happy, loving, and fulfilling relationship between (name of child) and (name of family member) for all the days of their lives. May there always be good communication between them and may unforgiveness have no root in their hearts.

Help them to love, value, appreciate, and respect one another so that the God-ordained tie between them cannot be broken.

Blessed are the peacemakers, for they shall be called sons of God.

Matthew 5:9

Prayer Notes

_____

_____

_____

_____

_____

_____

_____

_____

_____

_____

_____

Maintaining Good Family Relationships

Lord, I pray that You would teach my child to resolve misunderstandings according to Your Word. And if any division has already begun, if any relationship is strained or severed, Lord, I pray that You will drive out the wedge of division and bring healing. I pray that there be no strain, breach, misunderstanding, arguing, fighting, or separating of ties. Give her (him) a heart of forgiveness and reconciliation. Your Word instructs us to "be of one mind, having compassion for one another; love as brothers, be tenderhearted, be courteous" (1 Peter 3:8). Help her (him) to live accordingly, "endeavoring to keep the unity of the Spirit in the bond of peace" (Ephesians 4:3). In Jesus' name I pray that You would instill a love and compassion in her (him) for all family members that is strong and unending, like a cord that cannot be broken.

Behold, how good and how pleasant it is for brethren to dwell together in unity!

Psalm 133:1

Prayer Notes

_____

_____

_____

_____

_____

_____

_____

_____

_____

_____

_____

_____

Attracting Godly Friends and Role Models

Lord, I lift up (name of child) to You and ask that You would bring godly friends and role models into his (her) life. Give him (her) the wisdom he (she) needs to choose friends who are godly and help him (her) to never compromise his (her) walk with You in order to gain acceptance. Give me Holy Spirit-inspired discernment in how I guide or influence him (her) in the selection of friends. I pray that You would take anyone who is not a godly influence out of his (her) life or else transform that person into Your likeness. Your Word says, "He who walks with wise men will be wise, but the companion of fools will be destroyed" (Proverbs 13:20). Don't let my child be a companion of fools. Enable him (her) to walk with wise friends and not have to experience the destruction that can happen by walking with foolish people.

Make no friendship with an angry man, and with a furious man do not go, lest you learn his ways and set a snare for your soul.

Proverbs 22:24-25

Prayer Notes

Attracting Godly Friends and Role Models

Lord, I pray that You would deliver (name of child) from anyone in her life who has an ungodly character so that he (she) will not learn that person's ways and set a snare for his (her) own soul.

Whenever there is grief over a lost friendship, comfort him (her) and send new friends with whom he (she) can connect, share, and be the person You created him (her) to be.

Take away any loneliness or low self-esteem that would cause him (her) to seek out less than God-glorifying relationships. In Jesus' name I pray that You would teach him (her) the meaning of true friendship.

Teach him (her) how to be a good friend and make strong, close, lasting relationships. May each of his (her) friendships always glorify You.

Do not enter the path of the wicked, and do not walk in the way of evil.

Proverbs 4:14

Prayer Notes

_____

_____

_____

_____

_____

_____

_____

_____

_____

_____

Developing a Hunger for the Things of God

Lord, I pray for (name of child) to have an ever-increasing hunger for more of You. May she (he) long for Your presence—long to spend time with You in prayer, praise, and worship. Give her (him) a desire for the truth of Your Word and a love for Your laws and Your ways. Teach her (him) to live by faith and be led by the Holy Spirit, having an availability to do what You tell her (him) to do. May she (he) not have any allegiances or diversions away from You, but rather may she (he) be repulsed by ungodliness and all that is in opposition to You. May a deep reverence and love for You and Your ways color everything she (he) does and every choice she (he) makes. Help her (him) to understand the consequences of her (his) actions. May she (he) not be wise in her (his) own eyes, but rather "fear the LORD and depart from evil" (Proverbs 3:7).

Blessed are those who hunger and thirst for righteousness, for they shall be filled.

Matthew 5:6

Prayer Notes

Developing a Hunger for the Things of God

Lord, I pray that You will help (name of child) to be reliable, dependable, responsible, compassionate, sensitive, loving, and giving to others. Deliver her (him) from any pride, laziness, slothfulness, selfishness, or lust of the flesh. I pray that she (he) will have a teachable and submissive spirit, yet be able to stand strong in her (his) convictions. I pray that she (he) will always desire to belong to a Christian church that is alive to the truth of Your Word and the power of Holy Spirit-led worship and prayer. Write Your law in her (his) mind and on her (his) heart so that she (he) always walks with a confident assurance of the righteousness of Your commands. As she (he) learns to pray, teach her (him) to listen for Your voice. May there always be a Holy Spirit fire in her (his) heart and an unwavering desire for the things of God.

*Blessed are those who keep His testimonies, who
seek Him with the whole heart!*

Psalm 119:2

Prayer Notes

_____

_____

_____

_____

_____

_____

_____

_____

_____

_____

_____

_____

_____

Being the Person God Created

Lord, I pray that You would pour out Your Spirit upon (name of child) this day and anoint him (her) for all that You've called him (her) to be and do. May he (she) never stray from Your path and try to be something he (she) was not created to be.

Deliver him (her) from any evil plan of the devil to rob him (her) of life, to steal away his (her) uniqueness and giftedness, to compromise the path You've called him (her) to walk, or to destroy the person You created him (her) to be.

May he (she) not be a follower of anyone but You, but may he (she) be a leader of people into Your kingdom. May the fruit of the Spirit, which is love, joy, peace, patience, kindness, goodness, faithfulness, gentleness, and self-control, grow in him (her) daily (Galatians 5:22).

Be even more diligent to make your call and election sure, for if you do these things you will never stumble.

2 Peter 1:10

Prayer Notes

_____

_____

_____

_____

_____

_____

_____

_____

_____

_____

_____

Being the Person God Created

Lord, I pray that (name of child) will find his (her) identity in You. Help him (her) to view himself (herself) as Your instrument and know without doubt that in You he (she) is complete. Give him (her) a vision for his (her) life when setting goals for the future and a sense of purpose about what You've called him (her) to do. Help him (her) to see himself (herself) as You do—from his (her) future and not from his (her) past. Teach him (her) to look to You as his (her) hope for the future.

May he (she) understand it is You "who has saved us and called us with a holy calling, not according to our works, but according to His own purpose and grace which was given to us in Christ Jesus before time began" (2 Timothy 1:9).

May his (her) commitment to being who You created him (her) to be enable him (her) to grow daily in confidence and Holy Spirit boldness.

Eye has not seen, nor ear heard, nor have en-
tered into the heart of man the things which
God has prepared for those who love Him.

1 Corinthians 2:9

Prayer Notes

_____

_____

_____

_____

_____

_____

_____

_____

_____

_____

Following Truth, Rejecting Lies

Lord, I pray that You will fill (name of child) with Your Spirit of truth. Give her (him) a heart that loves truth and follows after it, rejecting all lies as a manifestation of the enemy.

Flush out anything in her (him) that would entertain a lying spirit and cleanse her (him) from any death that has crept in as a result of lies she (he) may have spoken or thought.

Help her (him) to understand that every lie gives the devil a piece of her (his) heart, and into the hole that's left comes confusion, death, and separation from Your presence.

Deliver her (him) from any lying spirit. I pray that she (he) not be blinded or deceived, but always be able to clearly understand Your truth.

Let not mercy and truth forsake you; bind them around your neck, write them on the tablet of your heart, and so find favor and high esteem in the sight of God and man.

Proverbs 3:3-4

Prayer Notes

_____

_____

_____

_____

_____

_____

_____

_____

_____

Following Truth, Rejecting Lies

Lord, I pray that (name of child) will never be able to get away with lying—that all lies will come to light and be exposed. If she (he) lies, may she (he) be so miserable that confession and its consequences will seem like a relief.

Help me to teach her (him) what it means to lie, and effectively discipline her (him) when she (he) tests that principle. Your Word says that "when He, the Spirit of truth, has come, He will guide you into all truth" (John 16:13).

I pray that Your Spirit of truth will guide her (him) into all truth. May she (he) never be a person who gives place to lies, but rather a person of integrity who follows hard after the Spirit of truth.

If you love Me, keep My commandments. And I will pray the Father, and He will give you another Helper, that He may abide with you forever—the Spirit of truth, whom the world cannot receive, because it neither sees Him nor knows Him; but you know Him, for He dwells with you and will be in you.

John 14:15-17

Prayer Notes

Enjoying a Life of Health and Healing

Lord, because You have instructed us in Your Word that we are to pray for one another so that we may be healed, I pray for healing and wholeness for (name of child). I pray that sickness and infirmity will have no place or power in his (her) life.

I pray for protection against any disease coming into his (her) body. Your Word says, "He sent His word and healed them, and delivered them from their destructions" (Psalm 107:20).

Wherever there is disease, illness, or infirmity in his (her) body, I pray that You, Lord, would touch him (her) with Your healing power and restore him (her) to total health.

Confess your trespasses to one another, and pray for one another, that you may be healed. The effective, fervent prayer of a righteous man avails much.

James 5:16

Prayer Notes

_____

_____

_____

_____

_____

_____

_____

_____

_____

Enjoying a Life of Health and Healing

Lord, I pray that You would deliver (name of child) from any destruction, disease, or injury that could come upon him (her).

Specifically I ask You to heal (name any specific problem). When and if we are to see a doctor, I pray that You, Lord, would show us who that should be. Give that doctor wisdom and full knowledge of the best way to proceed.

Thank You, Lord, that You suffered and died for us so that we might be healed. I lay claim to that heritage of healing which You have promised in Your Word and provided for those who believe. I look to You for a life of health, healing, and wholeness for my child.

But to you who fear My name the Sun of Righteousness shall arise with healing in His wings.

Malachi 4:2

Prayer Notes

_____

_____

_____

_____

_____

_____

_____

_____

_____

_____

_____

Having the Motivation for Proper Body Care

Lord, I lift (name of child) to You and ask that You would place in her (him) the desire to eat healthy food. Help her (him) to understand what's good for her (him) and what isn't, and give her (him) a desire for food that is healthful.

I pray that she (he) be spared from all eating disorders in any form. Along with the desire to eat properly, give her (him) the motivation to exercise regularly, to drink plenty of pure water, and to control and manage stress in her (his) life by living according to Your Word. Lord, Your Word says, "You shall know the truth, and the truth shall make you free" (John 8:32).

Help her (him) to see the truth about the way she (he) is to live, so that she (he) can be set free from any unhealthful habits.

Therefore, whether you eat or drink, or
whatever you do, do all for the glory of God.
1 Corinthians 10:31

Prayer Notes

_____

_____

_____

_____

_____

_____

_____

_____

_____

_____

Having the Motivation for Proper Body Care

Lord, I pray that You would give (name of child) a vision of her (his) body as the temple of the Holy Spirit. I pray that she (he) will value the body You've given her (him) and desire to take proper care of it. May she (he) not be critical of it, nor examine herself (himself) through the microscope of public opinion and acceptance.

I pray that she (he) will not be bound by the lure of fashion magazines, television, or movies which try to influence her (him) with an image of what they say she (he) should look like. Establish Your vision of health and attractiveness in her (his) heart this day. Help her (him) to see that what makes a person truly attractive is Your Holy Spirit living in her (him) and radiating outward. May she (he) come to understand that true attractiveness begins in the heart of one who loves God.

I beseech you therefore, brethren, by the mercies of God, that you present your bodies a living sacrifice, holy, acceptable to God, which is your reasonable service.

Romans 12:1

Prayer Notes

_____

_____

_____

_____

_____

_____

_____

_____

_____

_____

Instilling the Desire to Learn

Lord, I pray that (name of child) will have a deep reverence for You and Your ways. May he (she) hide Your Word in his (her) heart like a treasure, and seek after understanding like silver or gold. Give him (her) a good mind, a teachable spirit, and an ability to learn. Instill in him (her) a desire to attain knowledge and skill, and may he (she) have joy in the process.

Above all, I pray that he (she) will be taught by You, for Your Word says that when our children are taught by You they are guaranteed peace.

You have also said, "The fear of the LORD is the beginning of knowledge, but fools despise wisdom and instruction" (Proverbs 1:7). May he (she) never be a fool and turn away from learning, but rather may he (she) turn to You for the knowledge he (she) needs.

*All your children shall be taught by the LORD,
and great shall be the peace of your children.*
Isaiah 54:13

Prayer Notes

_____

_____

_____

_____

_____

_____

_____

_____

_____

_____

Instilling the Desire to Learn

Lord, I pray that (name of child) will respect the wisdom of his (her) parents and be willing to be taught by them. Bring the perfect teachers into his (her) life who are godly people from whom he (she) can easily learn. Let him (her) find favor with his (her) teachers and have good communication with them.

Help him (her) to excel in school and do well in any classes he (she) may take. Make the pathways of learning smooth and not something with which he (she) must strain and struggle.

Give him (her) clarity of thought, organization, good memory, and strong learning ability. I say to him (her) according to Your Word, "May the Lord give you understanding in all things" (2 Timothy 2:7).

Take firm hold of instruction, do not let go; keep her, for she is your life.

Proverbs 4:13

Prayer Notes

Identifying God-Given Gifts and Talents

Lord, I thank You for the gifts and talents You have placed in (name of child). I pray that You would develop them in her (him) and use them for Your glory. Make them apparent to me and to her (him), and show me specifically if there is any special nurturing, training, learning experience, or opportunities I should provide for her (him). May her (his) gifts and talents be developed in Your way and in Your time. Your Word says, "Having then gifts differing according to the grace that is given to us, let us use them" (Romans 12:6). As she (he) recognizes the talents and abilities You've given her (him), I pray that no feelings of inadequacy, fear, or uncertainty will keep her (him) from using them according to Your will. May she (he) hear the call You have on her (his) life so that she (he) doesn't spend a lifetime trying to figure out what it is or miss it altogether.

Every good gift and every perfect gift is from above, and comes down from the Father of lights, with whom there is no variation or shadow of turning.

James 1:17

Prayer Notes

_____

_____

_____

_____

_____

_____

_____

_____

_____

_____

Identifying God-Given Gifts and Talents

Lord, I pray that You would reveal to (name of child) what her (his) life work is to be and help her (him) excel in it.

Bless the work of her (his) hands, and may she (he) be able to earn a good living doing the work she (he) loves and does best. Let her (his) talent never be wasted, watered down by mediocrity, or used to glorify anything or anyone other than You, Lord. Your Word says that, "A man's gift makes room for him, and brings him before great men" (Proverbs 18:16).

May whatever she (he) does find favor with others and be well received and respected. But most of all, I pray the gifts and talents You placed in her (him) be released to find their fullest expression in glorifying You.

I thank my God always concerning you for the grace of God which was given to you by Christ Jesus, that you were enriched in every thing by Him in all utterance and all knowledge, even as the testimony of Christ was confirmed in you, so that you come short in no gift, eagerly waiting for the revelation of our Lord Jesus Christ.

1 Corinthians 1:4-7

Prayer Notes

Learning to Speak Life

Lord, I pray that (name of child) will choose to use speech that glorifies You. Fill his (her) heart with Your Spirit and Your truth so that what overflows from his (her) mouth will be words of life and not death. Put a monitor over his (her) mouth so that every temptation to use profane, negative, cruel, hurtful, uncaring, unloving, or compassionless language would pierce his (her) spirit and make him (her) feel uncomfortable.

I pray that obscene or foul language be so foreign to him (her) that if words like that ever do find their way through his (her) lips, they will be like gravel in his (her) mouth and he (she) will be repulsed by them.

Help him (her) to hear himself (herself) so that words don't come out carelessly or thoughtlessly. I pray that by his (her) words he (she) will be justified (Matthew 12:37).

A good man out of the good treasure of his heart
brings forth good things, and an evil man out
of the evil treasure brings forth evil things.

Matthew 12:35

Prayer Notes

Learning to Speak Life

Lord, I pray that You would keep (name of child) from being snared by the words of his (her) mouth. You've promised that "whoever guards his mouth and tongue keeps his soul from troubles" (Proverbs 21:23). Help him (her) to put a guard over his (her) mouth and keep far away from adversity.

Your Word says that "Death and life are in the power of the tongue, and those who love it will eat its fruit" (Proverbs 18:21). May he (she) speak life and not death. May he (she) be quick to listen and slow to speak so that his (her) speech will always be seasoned with grace. Equip him (her) to know how, what, and when to speak to anyone in any situation.

Enable him (her) to always speak words of hope, health, encouragement, and life, and to resolve that his (her) mouth will not sin.

Let the words of my mouth and the meditation of my heart be acceptable in Your sight, O LORD, my strength and my Redeemer.

Psalm 19:14

Prayer Notes

_____

_____

_____

_____

_____

_____

_____

_____

_____

_____

_____

Staying Attracted to Holiness and Purity

Lord, I pray that You would fill (name of child) with a love for You that surpasses her (his) love for anything or anyone else. Help her (him) to respect and revere Your laws and understand that they are there for her (his) benefit. May she (he) clearly see that when Your laws are disobeyed, life doesn't work.

Hide Your Word in her (his) heart so that there is no attraction to sin. I pray she (he) will run from evil, from impurity, from unholy thoughts, words, and deeds.

May she (he) be drawn toward whatever is pure and holy. Let Christ be formed in her (him) and cause her (him) to seek the power of Your Holy Spirit to enable her (him) to do what is right.

In a great house there are not only vessels of gold and silver, but also of wood and clay, some for honor and some for dishonor. Therefore if anyone cleanses himself from the latter, he will be a vessel of honor, sanctified and useful for the Master, prepared for every good work.

2 Timothy 2:20-21

Prayer Notes

Staying Attracted to Holiness and Purity

Lord, You have said, "Blessed are the pure in heart, for they shall see God" (Matthew 5:8). May a desire for holiness that comes from a pure heart be reflected in all that she (he) does. Let it be manifested in her (his) appearance as well.

I pray that the clothes she (he) wears and the way she (he) styles her (his) hair and chooses to adorn her (his) body and face will reflect a reverence and a desire to glorify You, Lord.

Where she (he) has strayed from the path of holiness, bring her (him) to repentance and work Your cleansing power in her (his) heart and life. Give her (him) understanding that to live in purity brings wholeness and blessing into her (his) life, and that the greatest reward for it is seeing You.

Who may ascend into the hill of the LORD? Or who may stand in His holy place? He who has clean hands and a pure heart, who has not lifted up his soul to an idol, nor sworn deceitfully. He shall receive blessing from the LORD, and righteousness from the God of his salvation.

Psalm 24:3-5

Prayer Notes

_____

_____

_____

_____

_____

_____

_____

Praying Through
a Child's Room

Lord, I invite Your Holy Spirit to dwell in this room, which belongs to (name of child). You are Lord over heaven and earth, and I proclaim that You are Lord over this room as well. Flood it with Your light and life.

Crowd out any darkness which seeks to impose itself here, and let no spirits of fear, depression, anger, doubt, anxiety, rebelliousness, or hatred (name anything you've seen manifested in your child's behavior) find any place here.

I pray that nothing will come into this room that is not brought by You, Lord. If there is anything here that shouldn't be, show me so it can be taken out. Give my child discernment about all that You find unacceptable.

Nor shall you bring an abomination into your house, lest you be doomed to destruction like it.
Deuteronomy 7:26

Prayer Notes

_____

_____

_____

_____

_____

_____

_____

_____

_____

_____

Praying Through a Child's Room

Lord, I pray that You would put Your complete protection over this room that belongs to (name of child) so that evil cannot enter here by any means. Fill his (her) room with Your love, peace, and joy. I pray that he (she) will say, as David did, "I will walk within my house with a perfect heart. I will set nothing wicked before my eyes" (Psalm 101:2-3).

I pray that You, Lord, will make this room a holy place, sanctified for Your glory. Cause him (her) to always want to cleanse himself "from all filthiness of the flesh and spirit, perfecting holiness in the fear of God" (2 Corinthians 7:1).

Lord, You have said that "The curse of the Lord is on the house of the wicked, but He blesses the home of the just" (Proverbs 3:33). Bless the habitation of this child.

Wash yourselves, make yourselves clean; put away the evil of your doings from before My eyes. Cease to do evil.

Isaiah 1:16

Prayer Notes

_____

_____

_____

_____

_____

_____

_____

_____

_____

_____

Enjoying Freedom from Fear

Lord, Your Word says, "I sought the LORD, and He heard me, and delivered me from all my fears" (Psalm 34:4). I seek You this day, believing that You hear me, and I pray that You will deliver (name of child) from any fear that threatens to overtake her (him). You said You have "not given us a spirit of fear, but of power and of love and of a sound mind" (2 Timothy 1:7).

Flood her (him) with Your love and wash away all fear and doubt. Give her (him) a sense of Your loving presence that far outweighs any fear that would threaten to overtake her (him).

Help her (him) to rely on Your power in such a manner that it establishes strong confidence and faith in You.

Fear not, for I am with you; be not dismayed, for I am your God. I will strengthen you, yes, I will help you, I will uphold you with My righteous right hand.

Isaiah 41:10

Prayer Notes

_____

_____

_____

_____

_____

_____

_____

_____

_____

Enjoying Freedom from Fear

Lord, You have said that "There is no fear in love; but perfect love casts out fear, because fear involves torment" (1 John 4:18). I pray that Your perfect love will surround (name of child) and give her (him) peace. Wherever there is real danger or good reason to fear, give her (him) wisdom, protect her (him) and draw her (him) close to You. Help her (him) not to deny her (his) fears, but take them to You in prayer and seek deliverance from them.

I pray that as she (he) draws close to You, Your love will penetrate her (his) life and crowd out all fear. Plant Your Word in her (his) heart. Let faith take root in her (his) mind and soul as she (he) grows in Your Word. Thank You, Lord, for Your promise to deliver us from all our fears. In Jesus' name I pray for freedom from fear on behalf of my child this day.

The LORD is the strength of my life; of whom shall I be afraid?

Psalm 27:1

Prayer Notes

_____

_____

_____

_____

_____

_____

_____

_____

_____

_____

_____

Receiving a Sound Mind

Lord, thank You for promising us a sound mind. I lay claim to that promise for (name of child). I pray that his (her) mind be clear, alert, bright, intelligent, stable, peaceful, and uncluttered. I pray there will be no confusion, no dullness, and no unbalanced, scattered, unorganized, or negative thinking.

I pray that his (her) mind will not be filled with complex or confusing thoughts. Rather, give him (her) clarity of mind so that he (she) is able to think straight at all times.

Give him (her) the ability to make clear decisions, to understand all he (she) needs to know, and to be able to focus on what he (she) needs to do. Where there is now any mental instability, I speak healing in Jesus' name.

God has not given us a spirit of fear, but of power and of love and of a sound mind.

2 Timothy 1:7

Prayer Notes

_____

_____

_____

_____

_____

_____

_____

_____

_____

_____

Receiving a Sound Mind

Lord, I pray that (name of child) will so love You with all his (her) heart, soul, and mind that there will be no room in him (her) for the lies of the enemy or the clamoring of the world.

May the Word of God take root in his (her) heart and fill his (her) mind with things that are true, noble, just, pure, lovely, of good report, virtuous, and praiseworthy (Philippians 4:8).

Give him (her) understanding that what goes into his (her) mind becomes part of him (her), so that he (she) will weigh carefully what he (she) sees and hears.

I pray that his (her) faith in You and Your Word will grow daily so that he (she) will live forever in peace and soundness of mind.

For to be carnally minded is death, but to be spiritually minded is life and peace.

Romans 8:6

Prayer Notes

Inviting the Joy of the Lord

Lord, I pray that (name of child) be given the gift of joy. Let the spirit of joy rise up in her (his) heart this day and may she (he) know the fullness of joy that is found only in Your presence. Help her (him) to understand that true happiness and joy are found only in You.

Whenever she (he) is overtaken by negative emotions, surround her (him) with Your love. Teach her (him) to say, "This is the day that the LORD has made, [I] will rejoice and be glad in it" (Psalm 118:24).

Deliver her (him) from despair, depression, loneliness, discouragement, anger, or rejection. May these negative attitudes have no place in (name of child), nor be a lasting part of her (his) life.

If you keep My commandments, you will abide in My love, just as I have kept My Father's commandments and abide in His love. These things I have spoken to you, that My joy may remain in you, and that your joy may be full.
John 15:10-11

Prayer Notes

Inviting the Joy of the Lord

Lord, I pray that You would plant Your Word firmly in (name of child). Etch it permanently on her (his) heart and increase her (his) faith daily. I know, Lord, that any negative emotions this child feels are lies, contrary to the truth of Your Word.

You have made her (him) to delight in You and not be anxious about anything. May she (he) decide in her (his) heart, "My soul shall be joyful in the LORD; it shall rejoice in His salvation" (Psalm 35:9).

I pray that You, the God of hope, will fill her (him) with joy and peace so that she (he) may abound in hope by the power of the Holy Spirit (Romans 15:13). Enable her (him) to abide in Your love and derive strength from the joy of knowing You this day and forever.

You will show me the path of life; in Your presence is fullness of joy; at Your right hand are pleasures forevermore.

Psalm 16:11

Prayer Notes

Destroying an Inheritance of Family Bondage

Lord, You have said in Your Word that a good man leaves an inheritance to his children's children (Proverbs 13:22). I pray that the inheritance I leave to my children will be the rewards of a godly life and a clean heart before You. To make sure that happens, I ask that wherever there is any kind of bondage in me that I have inherited from my family and accepted as mine, deliver me from it now in the name of Jesus. I confess the sins of my family to You. I don't even know what all of them are, but I know that You do. I ask for forgiveness and restoration. I also confess my own sins to You and ask for forgiveness, knowing Your Word says, "If we confess our sins, He is faithful and just to forgive us our sins and cleanse us from all unrighteousness" (1 John 1:9). I pray that no consequences of my sins be passed on to my child.

Therefore, if anyone is in Christ, he is a new creation; old things have passed away; behold, all things have become new.

2 Corinthians 5:17

Prayer Notes

_____

_____

_____

_____

_____

_____

_____

_____

_____

_____

Destroying an Inheritance of Family Bondage

Lord, I pray that no work of the enemy in my family's past will be able to encroach upon the life of my child, (name of child), today. I pray specifically about (name something you see in yourself or your family that you don't want passed on to your child). Whatever is not Your will for our lives, I reject as sin.

Thank You, Jesus, that You came to set us free from the past. We refuse to live bound by it. I pray that my son (daughter) will not inherit any bondage from his (her) earthly family, but will "inherit the kingdom prepared for him [her] from the foundation of the world" (Matthew 25:34).

Thank You, Jesus, that in You the old has passed away and all things are new.

Stand fast therefore in the liberty by which Christ has made us free, and do not be entangled again with a yoke of bondage.
Galatians 5:1

Prayer Notes

Avoiding Alcohol, Drugs, and Other Addictions

Lord, I pray that You would keep (name of child) free from any addiction—especially to alcohol or drugs. Make her (him) strong in You, draw her (him) close and enable her (him) to put You in control of her (his) life. Speak to her (his) heart, show her (him) the path she (he) should walk, and help her (him) see that protecting her (his) body from things that destroy it is a part of her (his) service to You.

Lord, You have said that "If you live according to the flesh you will die; but if by the Spirit you put to death the deeds of the body, you will live" (Romans 8:13). Teach her (him) to live by the Spirit and not the flesh.

*I have set before you life and death, blessing
and cursing; therefore choose life, that both you
and your descendants may live.*

Deuteronomy 30:19

Prayer Notes

_____

_____

_____

_____

_____

_____

_____

_____

_____

_____

Avoiding Alcohol, Drugs, and Other Addictions

Lord, I pray that You would thwart any plan Satan has to destroy her (his) life through alcohol and drugs. Take away anything in her (his) personality that would be drawn to those substances. Your Word says, "There is a way that seems right to a man, but its end is the way of death" (Proverbs 16: 25). Give her (him) discernment and strength to be able to say "no" to things that bring death and "yes" to the things of God that bring life.

May she (he) clearly see the truth whenever tempted and be delivered from the evil one whenever trapped. Enable her (him) to choose life in whatever she (he) does, and may her (his) only addiction be to the things of God. In Jesus' name I pray that everything she (he) does with her (his) body be done to Your glory.

The righteousness of the upright will deliver them, but the unfaithful will be caught by their lust.

Proverbs 11:6

Prayer Notes

_____

_____

_____

_____

_____

_____

_____

_____

_____

_____

Rejecting Sexual Immorality

Lord, I pray that You will keep (name of child) sexually pure all of his (her) life. Give him (her) a heart that wants to do what's right in this area, and let purity take root in his (her) personality and guide his (her) actions. Help him (her) to always lay down godly rules for relationships and resist anything that is not Your best.

Open his (her) eyes to the truth of Your Word, and help him (her) to see that sex outside of marriage will never be the committed, lasting, unconditional love that he (she) needs. Let his (her) personality not be scarred nor his (her) emotions damaged by the fragmentation of the soul that happens as a result of sexual immorality.

Put a Holy Spirit alarm in him (her) that goes off like a loud, flashing siren whenever he (she) steps over the line of what is right in Your sight.

This is the will of God, your sanctification: that you should abstain from sexual immorality.
1 Thessalonians 4:3

Prayer Notes

_____

_____

_____

_____

_____

_____

_____

_____

_____

_____

Rejecting Sexual Immorality

Lord, I pray that You would speak loudly to (name of child) whenever there is temptation to do something he (she) shouldn't, and make him (her) strong enough in You to stand for what's right. Help him (her) to resist temptation and say "no" to sexual immorality.

I pray that he (she) will have no premarital sex and no sex with anyone other than his (her) marriage partner.

I pray that homosexuality will never take root in him (her) or even have an opportunity to express itself toward him (her). Protect him (her) from any sexual molestation. May Your grace enable him (her) to be committed to staying pure so that he (she) will receive Your crown of life.

Blessed is the man who endures temptation; for when he has been approved, he will receive the crown of life which the Lord has promised to those who love Him.

James 1:12

Prayer Notes

Finding the Perfect Mate

Lord, I pray that unless Your plan is for (name of child) to remain single, You will send the perfect marriage partner for her (him). Send the right husband (wife) at the perfect time, and give her (him) a clear leading from You as to who it is.

I pray that my daughter (son) will be submissive enough to hear Your voice when it comes time to make a marriage decision, and that she (he) will make that decision based on what You are saying and not just fleshly desire.

I pray that she (he) will trust You with all her (his) heart and lean not on her (his) own understanding; that she (he) will acknowledge You in all her (his) ways so that You will direct her (his) path (Proverbs 3:5-6). May she (he) have one wonderful mate for life.

Whoever divorces his wife and marries another
commits adultery against her.

Mark 10:11

Prayer Notes

_____

_____

_____

_____

_____

_____

_____

_____

_____

_____

_____

_____

Finding the Perfect Mate

Lord, I pray that You would prepare the person who will make the perfect husband (wife) for (name of child). Help her (him) to know the difference between simply falling in love and knowing for certain this is the person with whom God wants her (him) to spend the rest of her (his) life. If she (he) becomes attracted to someone she (he) shouldn't marry, I pray that You, Lord, would cut off the relationship.

I pray that she (he) will marry a godly and devoted servant of Yours, who loves You and lives Your way, and will be a blessing to all other family members. May they be mutually loyal, compassionate, considerate, sensitive, respectful, affectionate, forgiving, supportive, caring, and loving toward one another all the days of their lives.

There are many plans in a man's heart, never-theless the LORD's counsel—that will stand.
Proverbs 19:21

Prayer Notes

Living Free of Unforgiveness

Lord, I pray that You would enable (name of child) to live in ongoing forgiveness. Teach him (her) the depth of your forgiveness toward him (her) so that he (she) can be freely forgiving toward others. Help him (her) to make the decision to forgive based on what You've asked us to do and not on what feels good at the moment.

May he (she) understand that forgiveness doesn't justify the other person's actions; instead, it makes him (her) free. Help him (her) to understand that only You know the whole story about any of us, and that's why he (she) doesn't have the right to judge.

Teach him (her) to release the past to You so that he (she) can move into all that You have for him (her).

Let all bitterness, wrath, anger, clamor, and evil speaking be put away from you, with all malice. And be kind to one another, tenderhearted, forgiving one another, even as God in Christ forgave you.

Ephesians 4:31-32

Prayer Notes

Living Free of Unforgiveness

Lord, I pray that (name of child) will never harbor resentment, bitterness, anger, or unforgiveness toward anyone. Help him (her) to recognize these feelings immediately whenever they creep in, and enable him (her) to release them to You.

I also pray that he (she) will forgive himself (herself) for times of failure, and may he (she) never blame You, Lord, for things that happen on this earth and in his (her) life. According to Your Word I pray that he (she) will love his (her) enemies, bless those who curse him (her), do good to those who hate him (her), and pray for those who spitefully use and persecute him (her), so that he (she) may enjoy all Your blessings (Matthew 5:44-45).

In Jesus' name, I pray that he (she) will live in the fullness of Your forgiveness for him (her) and the freedom of forgiveness toward others.

Whenever you stand praying, if you have anything against anyone, forgive him, that your Father in heaven may also forgive you your trespasses.

Mark 11:25

Prayer Notes

_____

_____

_____

_____

_____

_____

_____

_____

_____

_____

Walking in Repentance

Lord, I pray that You would give (name of child) a heart that is quick to confess her (his) mistakes. May she (he) be truly repentant of them so that she (he) can be forgiven and cleansed. Help her (him) to understand that Your laws are for her (his) benefit and that the confession and repentance You require must become a way of life.

Give her (him) the desire to live in truth before You, and may she (he) say as David did, "Wash me thoroughly from my iniquity, and cleanse me from my sin…Create in me a clean heart, O God, and renew a steadfast spirit within me. Do not cast me away from Your presence, and do not take Your Holy Spirit from me. Restore to me the joy of Your salvation" (Psalm 51:2,10-12).

He who covers his sins will not prosper, but whoever confesses and forsakes them will have mercy.

Proverbs 28:13

Prayer Notes

_____

_____

_____

_____

_____

_____

_____

_____

_____

_____

_____

Walking in Repentance

Lord, I pray that You would bring to light any hidden sins in (name of child) so they can be confessed, repented of, and forgiven. Your Word says, "Blessed is he whose transgression is forgiven, whose sin is covered" (Psalm 32:1).

I pray that my daughter (son) will never be able to contain sin within her (him), but rather let there be a longing to confess fully and say, "See if there is any wicked way in me, and lead me in the way everlasting" (Psalm 139:24).

May she (he) not live in guilt and condemnation, but rather dwell with a clear conscience in the full understanding of her (his) forgiveness in Christ. I pray that she (he) will always look to You and wear a radiant countenance.

Beloved, if our heart does not condemn us, we have confidence toward God. And whatever we ask we receive from Him, because we keep His commandments and do those things that are pleasing in His sight.

1 John 3:21-22

Prayer Notes

_____

_____

_____

_____

_____

_____

_____

_____

_____

Breaking Down Ungodly Strongholds

Lord, I thank You that You have promised in Your Word to deliver us when we cry out to You. I come to You on behalf of (name of child) and ask that You would deliver him (her) from any ungodliness that may be threatening to become a stronghold in his (her) life.

Even though I don't know what he (she) needs to be set free from, You do. I pray in the name of Jesus that You will work deliverance in his (her) life wherever it is needed. I know that although "we walk in the flesh, we do not war according to the flesh. For the weapons of our warfare are not carnal but mighty in God for pulling down strongholds, casting down arguments and every high thing that exalts itself against the knowledge of God" (2 Corinthians 10:3-5). I depend on You, Lord, to give me wisdom and revelation. Show me anything I need to see regarding him (her).

There is nothing covered that will not be revealed, and hidden that will not be known.

Matthew 10:26

Prayer Notes

_____

_____

_____

_____

_____

_____

_____

_____

_____

_____

Breaking Down Ungodly Strongholds

Lord, I put (name of child) in Your hands this day. Guide, protect, and convict him (her) when sin is trying to take root. Strengthen him (her) in battle when Satan attempts to gain a foothold in his (her) heart. Make him (her) sensitive to enemy encroachment, and may he (she) run to You to be his (her) stronghold and refuge in times of trouble.

May the cry of his (her) heart be, "Cleanse me from secret faults" (Psalm 19:12). According to Your Word I say that You, Lord, will deliver him (her) from every evil work and preserve him (her) for Your heavenly kingdom (2 Timothy 4:18).

Let all that is hidden come to light. If there is any action I need to take, I depend on You to show me. Thank You that You help me parent this child.

I will give you the keys of the kingdom of heaven, and whatever you bind on earth will be bound in heaven, and whatever you loose on earth will be loosed in heaven.

Matthew 16:19

Prayer Notes

_____

_____

_____

_____

_____

_____

_____

_____

_____

Seeking Godly Wisdom and Discernment

Lord, I pray that You would give the gifts of wisdom, discernment, and revelation to (name of child). Help her (him) to trust You with all her (his) heart, not depending on her (his) own understanding, but acknowledging You in all her (his) ways so that she (he) may hear Your clear direction as to which path to take (Proverbs 3:5-6).

Help her (him) to discern good from evil and be sensitive to the voice of the Holy Spirit saying, "This is the way, walk in it" (Isaiah 30:21).

I know that much of her (his) happiness in life depends on gaining wisdom and discernment, which Your Word says brings long life, wealth, recognition, protection, enjoyment, contentment, and happiness. May all these things come to her (him) because of Your gift of wisdom.

A wise son makes a glad father, but a foolish son is the grief of his mother.

Proverbs 10:1

Prayer Notes

_____

_____

_____

_____

_____

_____

_____

_____

_____

_____

_____

Seeking Godly Wisdom and Discernment

Lord, Your Word says, "The fear of the LORD is the beginning of wisdom, and the knowledge of the Holy One is understanding" (Proverbs 9:10). May a healthy fear and knowledge of You be the foundation upon which wisdom and discernment are established in (name of child).

May she (he) turn to You for all decisions so that she (he) doesn't make poor choices. Help her (him) to see that all the treasures of wisdom and knowledge are hidden in You and that You give of them freely when we ask for them.

As she (he) seeks wisdom and discernment from You, Lord, pour it liberally upon her (him) so that all her (his) paths will be peace and life.

Happy is the man who finds wisdom, and the man who gains understanding; for her proceeds are better than the profits of silver, and her gain than fine gold.

Proverbs 3:13-14

Prayer Notes

_____

_____

_____

_____

_____

_____

_____

_____

_____

Growing in Faith

Lord, You have said in Your Word that You have "dealt to each one a measure of faith" (Romans 12:3). I pray that You would take the faith You have planted in (name of child) and multiply it. May the truth of Your Word be firmly established in his (her) heart so that faith will grow daily and navigate his (her) life. Help him (her) to trust You at all times as he (she) looks to You for truth, guidance, and transformation into Your likeness. May his (her) faith be the "substance of things hoped for, the evidence of things not seen" (Hebrews 11:1).

I pray he (she) will have faith strong enough to lift him (her) above his (her) circumstances and limitations and instill in him (her) the confidence of knowing that everything will work together for good.

Whatever things you ask when you pray, believe that you receive them, and you will have them.

Mark 11:24

Prayer Notes

_____

_____

_____

_____

_____

_____

_____

_____

_____

_____

Growing in Faith

Lord, I pray that (name of child) will be so strong in faith that his (her) relationship with You supersedes all else in his (her) life—even my influence as a parent. In other words, may he (she) have a relationship with You, Lord, that is truly his (her) own—not an extension of mine or anyone else's.

I want the comfort of knowing that when I'm no longer on this earth, his (her) faith will be strong enough to keep him (her) "steadfast, immovable, always abounding in the work of the Lord" (1 Corinthians 15:58).

I pray that he (she) will take the "shield of faith" in order to "quench all the fiery darts of the wicked one" (Ephesians 6:16).

If you have faith as a mustard seed, you will say to this mountain, "Move from here to there," and it will move; and nothing will be impossible for you.
                                    Matthew 17:20

Prayer Notes

_____

_____

_____

_____

_____

_____

_____

_____

_____

Other Books
by Stormie Omartian

The Power of a Praying® Woman

Stormie Omartian's bestselling books have helped hundreds of thousands of individuals pray more effectively for their spouses, their children, and their nation. Now she has written a book on a subject she knows intimately: being a praying woman. Stormie's deep knowledge of Scripture and candid examples from her own prayer life provide guidance for women who seek to trust God with deep longings and cover every area of life with prayer.

The Power of a Praying® Wife

Stormie shares how wives can develop a deeper relationship with their husbands by praying for them. With this practical advice on praying for specific areas, including decision-making, fears, spiritual strength, and sexuality, women will discover the fulfilling marriage God intended.

The Power of a Praying® Husband

Building on the success of *The Power of a Praying® Wife,* Stormie offers this guide to help husbands pray more effectively for their wives. Each chapter features comments from well-known Christian men, biblical wisdom, and prayer ideas.

The Power of a Praying® Parent

This powerful book for parents offers 30 easy-to-read chapters that focus on specific areas of prayers for children. This personal, practical guide leads the way to enriched, strong prayer lives for both moms and dads.

Just Enough Light for the Step I'm On

New Christians and those experiencing life changes or difficult times will appreciate Stormie's honesty, candor, and advice based on experience and the Word of God in this collection of devotional readings perfect for the pressures of today's world.